LEARN TO DRAW... FACES

By Mara Conlon

Illustrated by Kerren Barbas Steckler

Designed by Heather Zschock

PETER PAUPER PRESS, INC.

White Plains, New York

For Copeland, Emily, Audrey, and Jake

PETER PAUPER PRESS

In 1928, at the age of twenty-two, Peter Beilenson began printing books on a small press in the basement of his parents' home in Larchmont, New York. Peter—and later, his wife, Edna—sought to create fine books that sold at "prices even a pauper could afford."

Today, still family owned and operated, Peter Pauper Press continues to honor our founders' legacy of quality, value, and fun for big kids and small kids alike.

Illustrations copyright © 2019 Kerren Barbas Steckler
Designed by Heather Zschock

Copyright © 2019
Peter Pauper Press, Inc.
Manufactured for Peter Pauper Press, Inc.
202 Mamaroneck Avenue
White Plains, NY 10601 USA
All rights reserved
ISBN 978-1-4413-3075-8
Printed in China

Published in the United Kingdom and Europe by
Peter Pauper Press, Inc. c/o White Pebble International
Unit 2, Plot 11 Terminus Road
Chichester, West Sussex PO19 8TX, UK

Visit us at www.peterpauper.com

Hey, young artists!

Are you ready to learn how to draw over 40 different faces? It's easy and fun! Just follow these steps:

First, pick a face you want to draw.

Next, trace over the face with a pencil. This will give you a feel for how to draw the lines.

Then, following the numbered boxes, start drawing each new step (**shown in red**) on each left-side page to draw the face on top of the basic shapes provided on each right-side page. There is also empty space on the page provided for you to draw the face from scratch! Each face also has variations included for different expressions, or accessories.

Lastly, if you're an awesome artist (and of course, you are!), try drawing a whole bunch of people's faces together. And remember, don't worry if your drawings look different from the ones in this book—no two faces are exactly alike!

You're on your way to creating your own special masterpieces!

GET READY! GET SET! DRAW!

Emotions

Serious

Friendly

Happy

Laughing

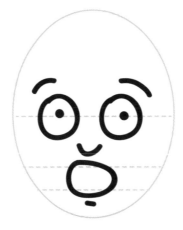

Scared

Sad

Sneaky

Suspicious

Angry

Try drawing all of the different emotions!

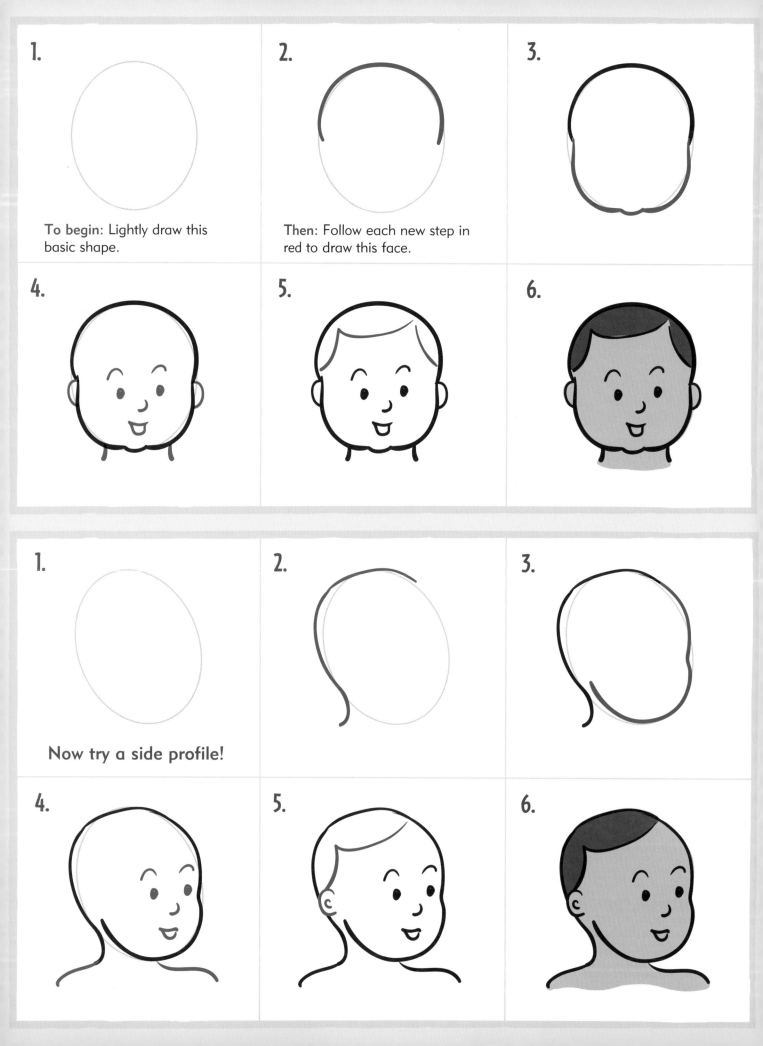

1.
To begin: Lightly draw this basic shape.

2.
Then: Follow each new step in red to draw this face.

3.

4.

5.

6.

1.
Now try a side profile!

2.

3.

4.

5.

6.

First, trace over each face to practice!

Then, try drawing your own faces over the basic shapes!

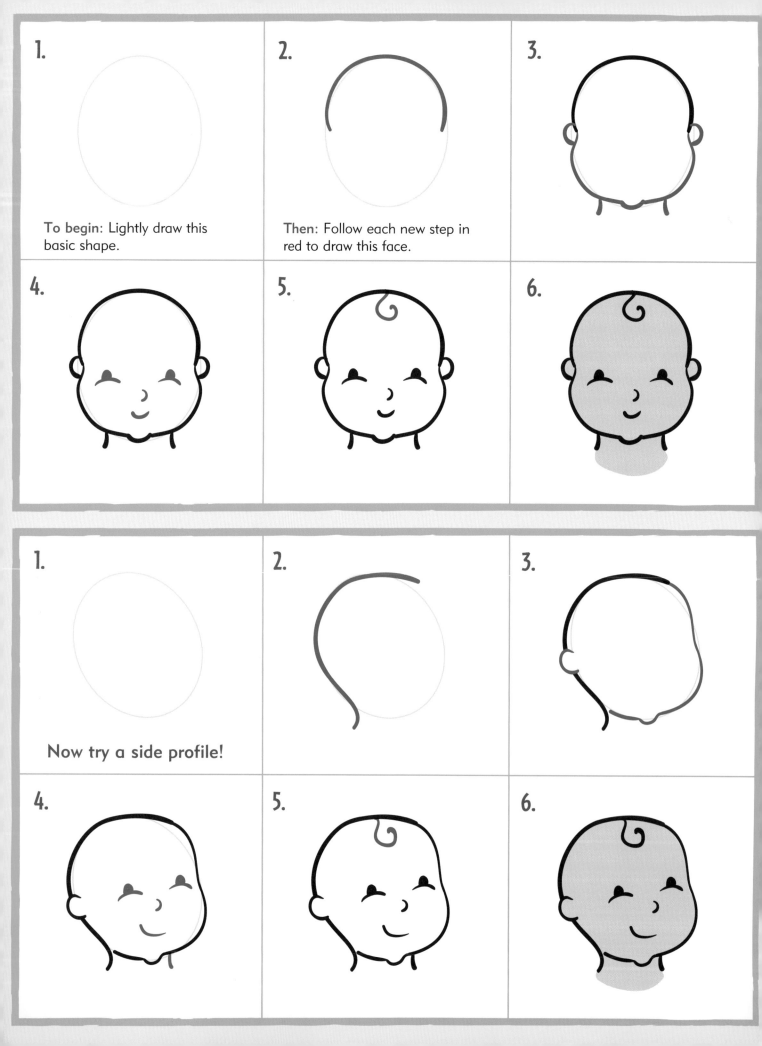

1.

To begin: Lightly draw this basic shape.

2.

Then: Follow each new step in red to draw this face.

3.

4.

5.

6.

1.

Now try a side profile!

2.

3.

4.

5.

6.

First, trace over each face to practice!

Then, try drawing your own faces over the basic shapes!

1.

To begin: Lightly draw this basic shape.

2.

Then: Follow each new step in red to draw this face.

3.

4.

5.

6.

1.

Now try a side profile!

2.

3.

4.

5.

6.

First, trace over each face to practice!

Then, try drawing your own faces over the basic shapes!

1.
To begin: Lightly draw this basic shape.

2.
Then: Follow each new step in red to draw this face.

3.

4.

5.

6.

1.
Now try a side profile!

2.

3.

4.

5.

6.

First, trace over each face to practice!

Then, try drawing your own faces over the basic shapes!

1.

To begin: Lightly draw this basic shape.

2.

Then: Follow each new step in red to draw this face.

3.

4.

5.

6.

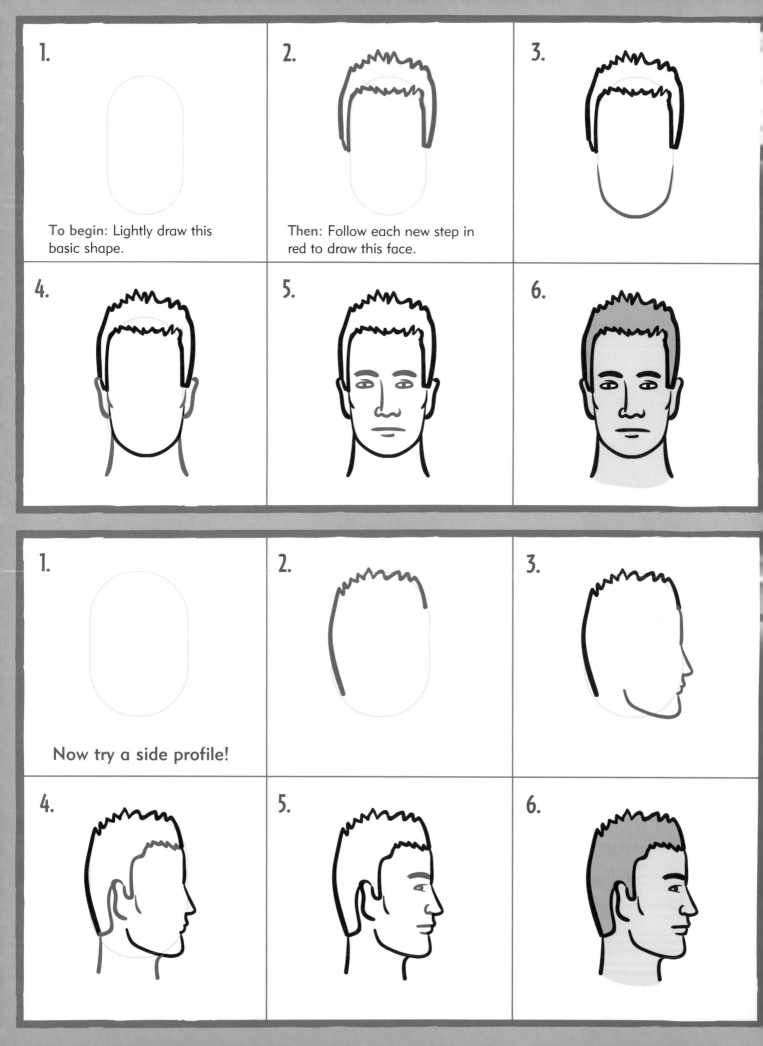

1.

Now try a side profile!

2.

3.

4.

5.

6.

First, trace over each face to practice!

Then, try drawing your own faces over the basic shapes!

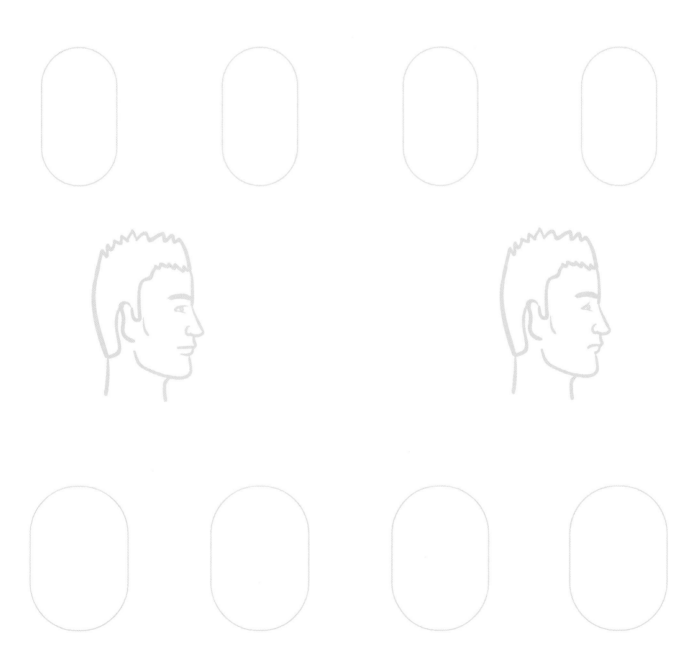

1.

To begin: Lightly draw this basic shape.

2.

Then: Follow each new step in red to draw this face.

3.

4.

5.

6.

1.

Now try a side profile!

2.

3.

4.

5.

6.

First, trace over each face to practice!

Then, try drawing your own faces over the basic shapes!

1.

To begin: Lightly draw this basic shape.

2.

Then: Follow each new step in red to draw this face.

3.

4.

5.

6.

1.

Now try a side profile!

2.

3.

4.

5.

6.

First, trace over each face to practice!

Then, try drawing your own faces over the basic shapes!

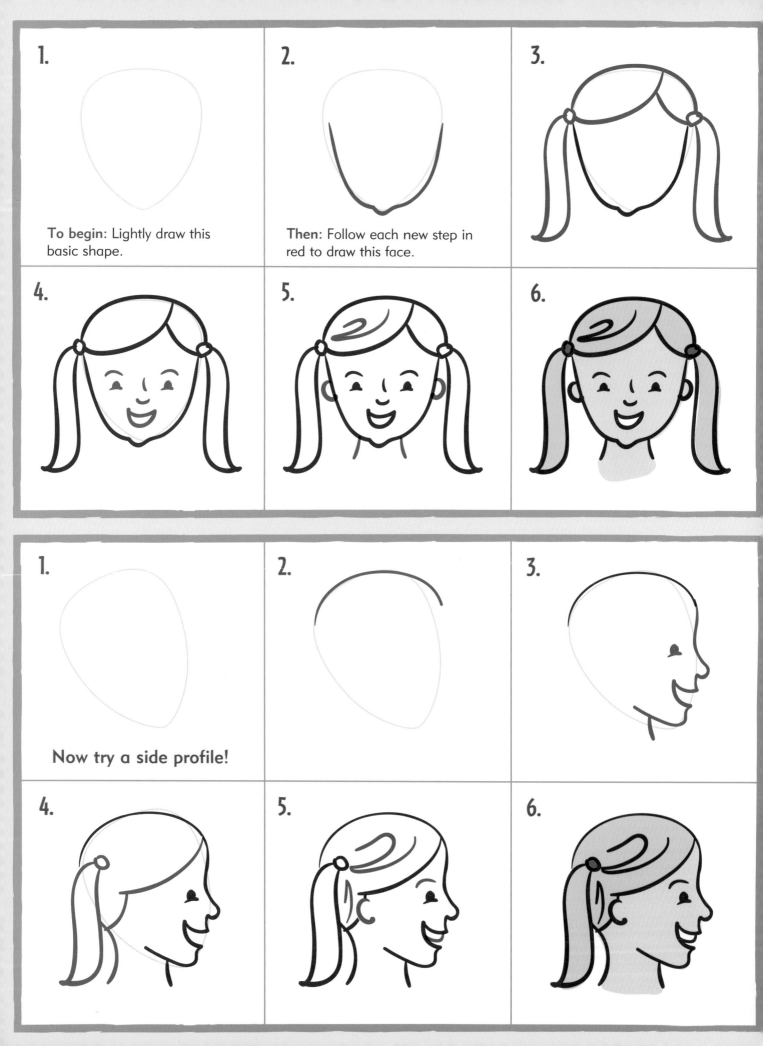

1.

To begin: Lightly draw this basic shape.

2.

Then: Follow each new step in red to draw this face.

3.

4.

5.

6.

1.

Now try a side profile!

2.

3.

4.

5.

6.

First, trace over each face to practice!

Then, try drawing your own faces over the basic shapes!

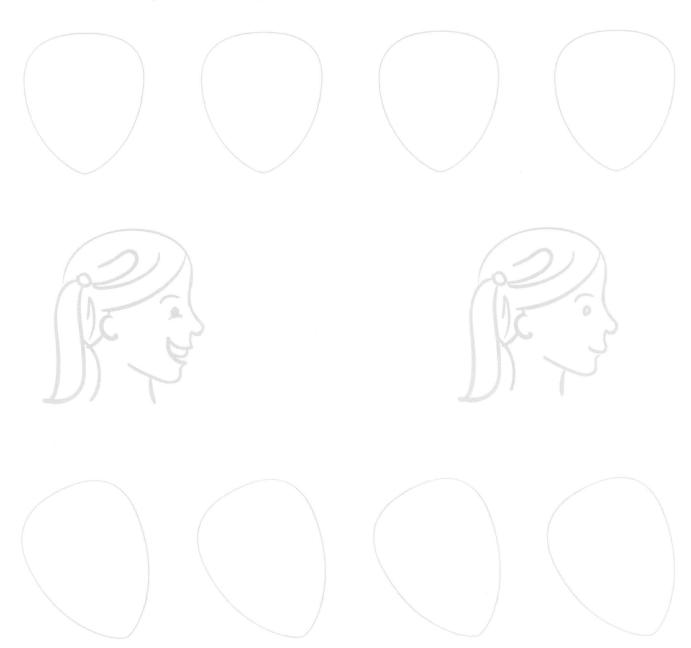

1.

To begin: Lightly draw this basic shape.

2.

Then: Follow each new step in red to draw this face.

3.

4.

5.

6.

1.

Now try a side profile!

2.

3.

4.

5.

6.

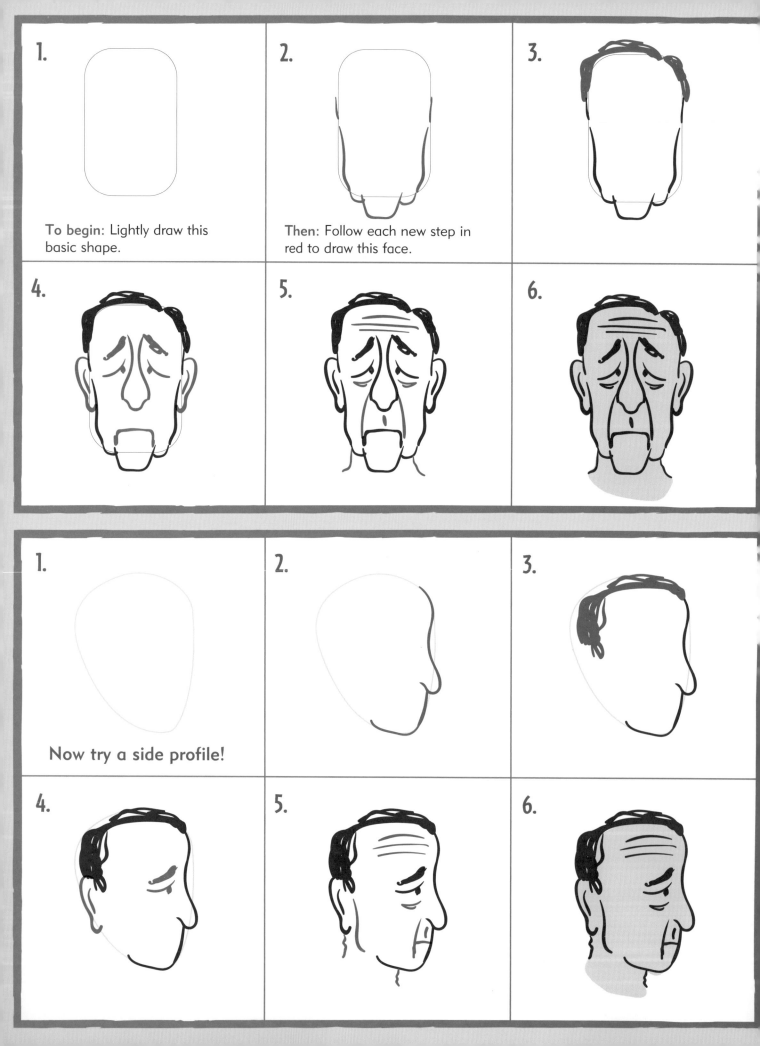

First, trace over each face to practice!

Then, try drawing your own faces over the basic shapes!

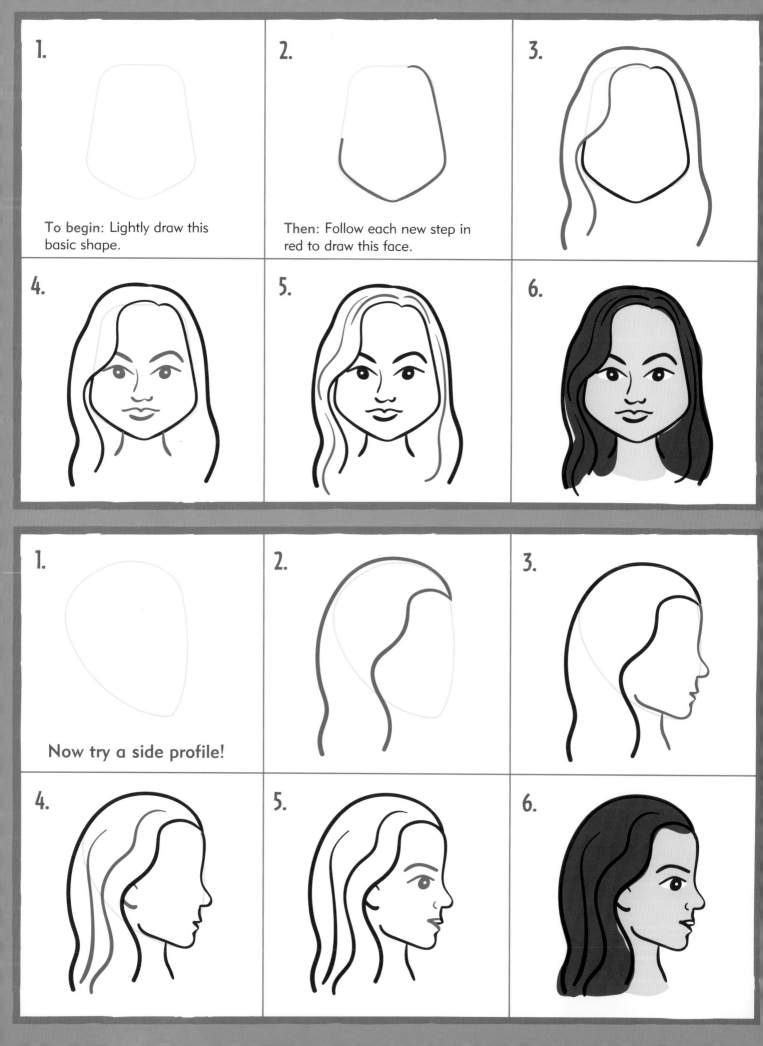

1.
To begin: Lightly draw this basic shape.

2.
Then: Follow each new step in red to draw this face.

3.

4.

5.

6.

1.
Now try a side profile!

2.

3.

4.

5.

6.

Then, try drawing your own faces over the basic shapes!

1.

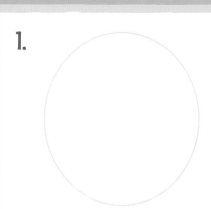

To begin: Lightly draw this basic shape.

2.

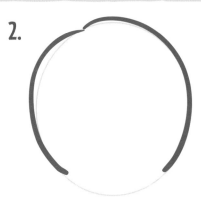

Then: Follow each new step in red to draw this face.

3.

4.

5.

6.

1.

Now try a side profile!

2.

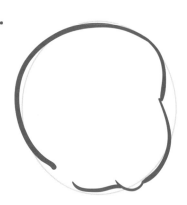

3.

4.

5.

6.

First, trace over each face to practice!

Then, try drawing your own faces over the basic shapes!

1.

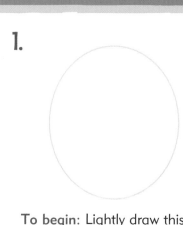

To begin: Lightly draw this basic shape.

2.

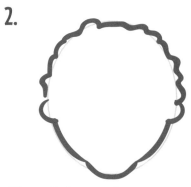

Then: Follow each new step in red to draw this face.

3.

4.

5.

6.

1.

Now try a side profile!

2.

3.

4.

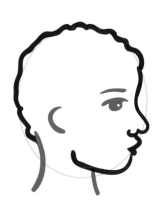

5.

6.

First, trace over each face to practice!

Then, try drawing your own faces over the basic shapes!

1.

To begin: Lightly draw this basic shape.

2.

Then: Follow each new step in red to draw this face.

3.

4.

5.

6.

1.

Now try a side profile!

2.

3.

4.

5.

6.

First, trace over each face to practice!

Then, try drawing your own faces over the basic shapes!

1.

To begin: Lightly draw this basic shape.

2.

Then: Follow each new step in red to draw this face.

3.

4.

5.

6.

1.

Now try a side profile!

2.

3.

4.

5.

6.

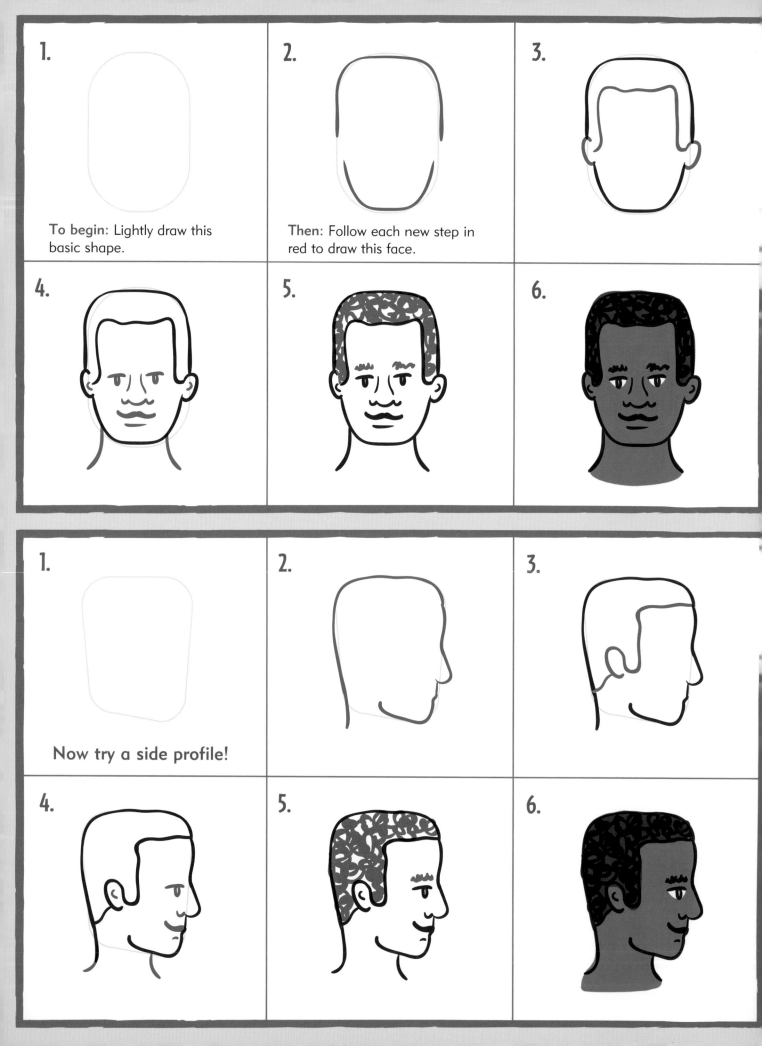

First, trace over each face to practice!

Then, try drawing your own faces over the basic shapes!

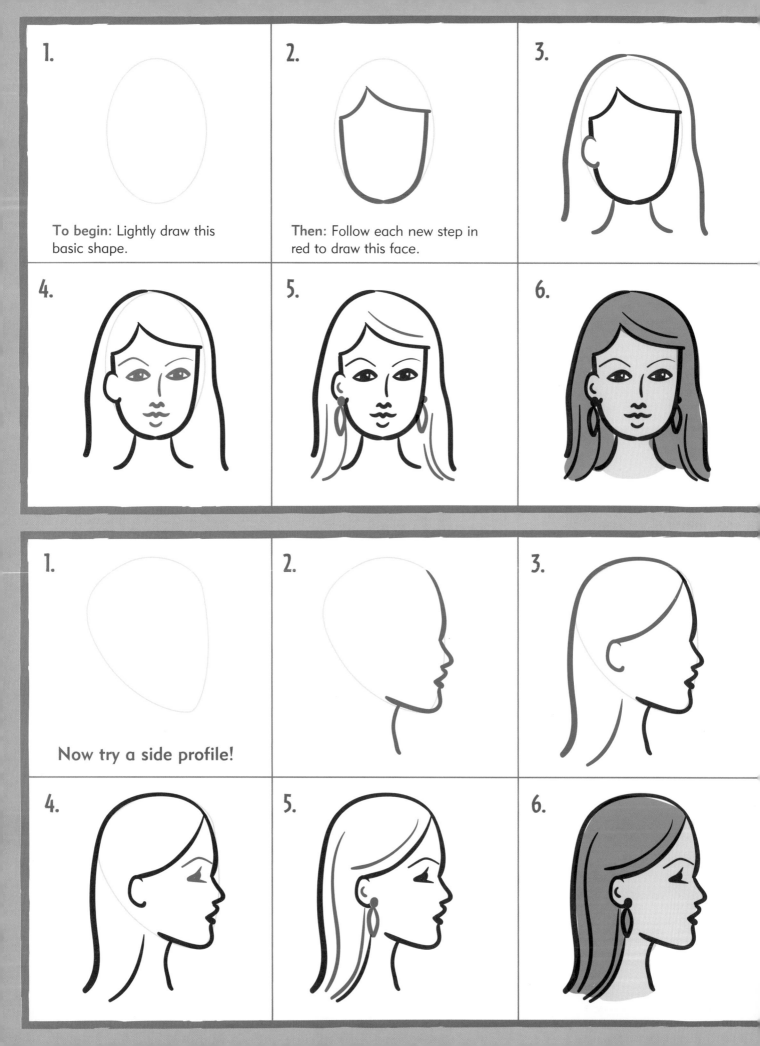

1.
To begin: Lightly draw this basic shape.

2.
Then: Follow each new step in red to draw this face.

3.

4.

5.

6.

1.
Now try a side profile!

2.

3.

4.

5.

6.

Then, try drawing your own faces over the basic shapes!

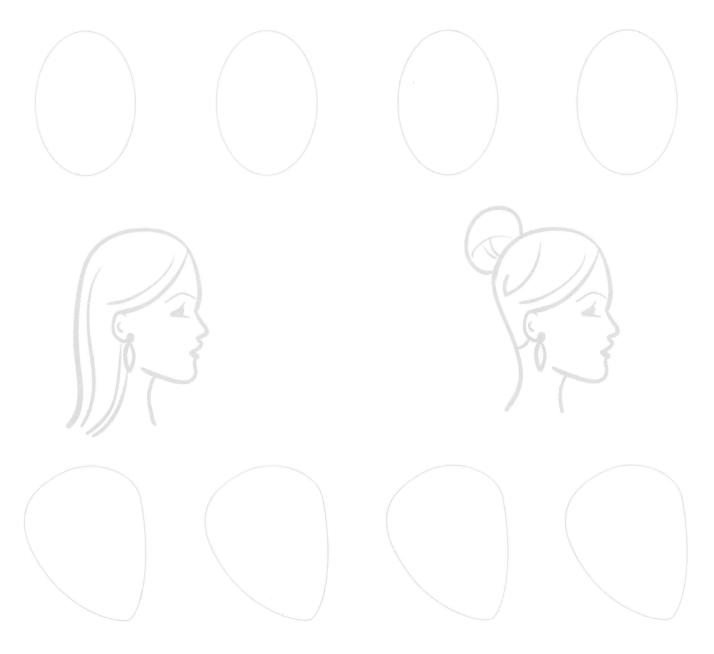

1.

To begin: Lightly draw this basic shape.

2.

Then: Follow each new step in red to draw this face.

3.

4.

5.

6.

1.

Now try a side profile!

2.

3.

4.

5.

6.

First, trace over each face to practice!

Then, try drawing your own faces over the basic shapes!

1.
To begin: Lightly draw this basic shape.

2.
Then: Follow each new step in red to draw this face.

3.

4.

5.

6.

1.
Now try a side profile!

2.

3.

4.

5.

6.

First, trace over each face to practice!

Then, try drawing your own faces over the basic shapes!

1.

To begin: Lightly draw this basic shape.

2.

Then: Follow each new step in red to draw this face.

3.

4.

5.

6.

1.

Now try a side profile!

2.

3.

4.

5.

6.

First, trace over each face to practice!

Then, try drawing your own faces over the basic shapes!

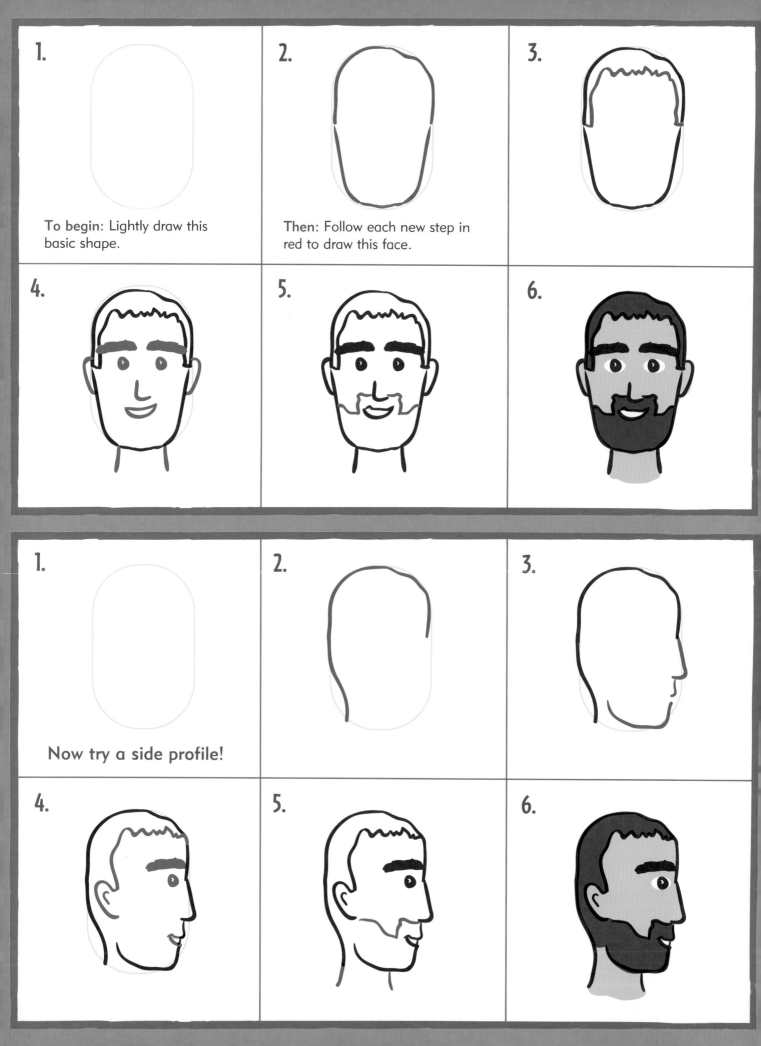

1.
To begin: Lightly draw this basic shape.

2.
Then: Follow each new step in red to draw this face.

3.

4.

5.

6.

1.
Now try a side profile!

2.

3.

4.

5.

6.

First, trace over each face to practice!

Then, try drawing your own faces over the basic shapes!

1. To begin: Lightly draw this basic shape.

2. Then: Follow each new step in red to draw this face.

3.

4.

5.

6.

1. Now try a side profile!

2.

3.

4.

5.

6.

First, trace over each face to practice!

Then, try drawing your own faces over the basic shapes!

1.

To begin: Lightly draw this basic shape.

2.

Then: Follow each new step in red to draw this face.

3.

4.

5.

6.

1.

Now try a side profile!

2.

3.

4.

5.

6.

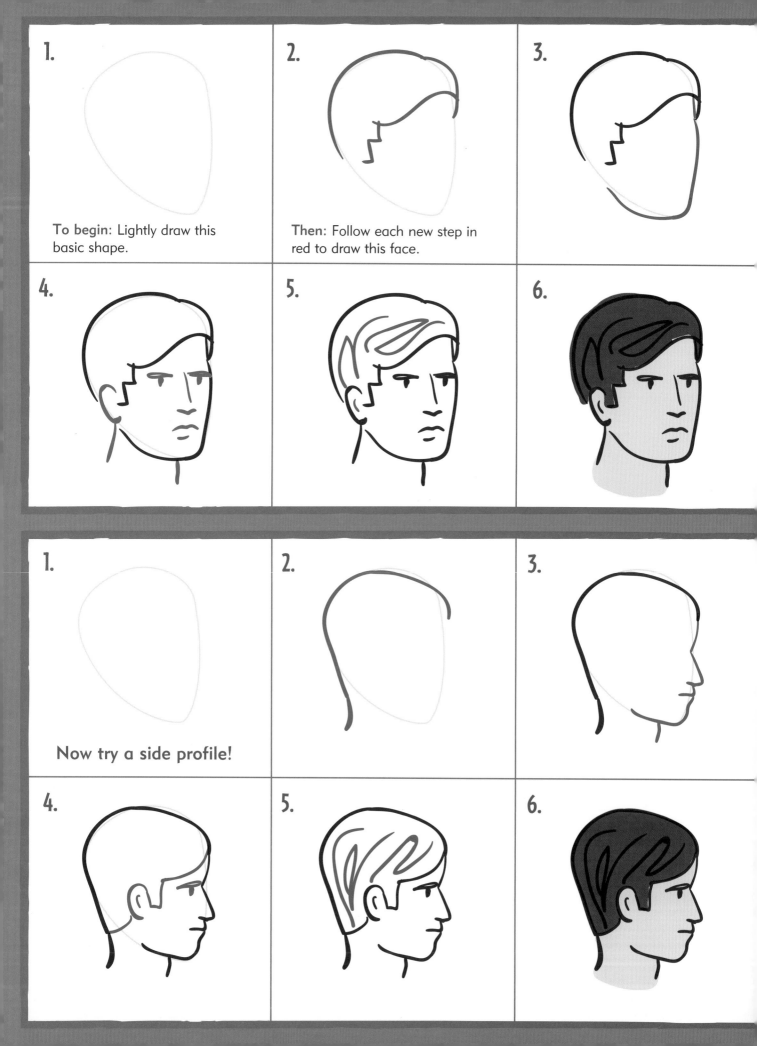

First, trace over each face to practice!

Then, try drawing your own faces over the basic shapes!

We've reached the end,
and now we're done.

Drawing faces
is so much fun!